CLAYTON KERSHAW

Cliff Mills

Mitchell Lane

PUBLISHERS

P.O. Box 196
Hockessin, Delaware 19707
Visit us on the web: www.mitchelllane.com
Comments? Email us: mitchelllane@mitchelllane.com

Printing   1   2   3   4   5   6   7   8   9

A Robbie Reader Biography

Abigail Breslin
Adrian Peterson
Albert Einstein
Albert Pujols
Aly and AJ
Andrew Luck
AnnaSophia Robb
Ashley Tisdale
Brenda Song
Brittany Murphy
Buster Posey
Charles Schulz
Chris Johnson
Clayton Kershaw
Cliff Lee
Colin Kaepernick
Dale Earnhardt Jr.
Darius Rucker
David Archuleta

Demi Lovato
Donovan McNabb
Drake Bell & Josh Peck
Dr. Seuss
Dustin Pedroia
Dwayne "The Rock" Johnson
Dwyane Wade
Dylan & Cole Sprouse
Emily Osment
Hilary Duff
Jamie Lynn Spears
Jennette McCurdy
Jesse McCartney
Jimmie Johnson
Joe Flacco
Jonas Brothers
Keke Palmer
Larry Fitzgerald

LeBron James
Mia Hamm
Miguel Cabrera
Miley Cyrus
Miranda Cosgrove
Philo Farnsworth
Raven-Symoné
Robert Griffin III
Roy Halladay
Shaquille O'Neal
Story of Harley-Davidson
Sue Bird
Syd Hoff
Tiki Barber
Tim Lincecum
Tom Brady
Tony Hawk
Troy Polamalu
Victor Cruz
Victoria Justice

Library of Congress Cataloging-in-Publication Data
Mills, Cliff, 1947–
Clayton Kershaw / by Cliff Mills.
    pages cm. — (A Robbie reader)
Includes bibliographical references and index.
ISBN 978-1-61228-636-5 (library bound)
1. Kershaw, Clayton. 2. Pitchers (Baseball)—United States—Biography—Juvenile literature. 3. Baseball players—United States—Biography—Juvenile literature. I. Title.
GV865.K47M45 2015
796.357092—dc23
[B]
2014008317

eBook ISBN: 9781612286617

ABOUT THE AUTHOR: Cliff Mills has written several books about sports figures, including Derek Jeter, Curt Schilling, Bernie Williams, Tony Romo, and Adrian Peterson. He lives in Jacksonville, Florida, with his wife, a landscaper. He is a long-time Red Sox fan, but rooted for the Dodgers when he lived in Los Angeles.

TABLE OF CONTENTS

Words in bold type can be found in the glossary.

Clayton Kershaw throws with power during his perfect inning at the 2011 All-Star Game in Phoenix, Arizona.

A Battle Between the Best

Major League Baseball's annual All-Star Game is a battle of the best pitchers against the best hitters. With the National League leading 3–1 at the start of the fifth inning of the 2011 All-Star Game in Phoenix, Arizona, Clayton Kershaw of the Los Angeles Dodgers jogged to the mound. Many people in the crowd cheered for the 23-year-old pitcher. He was appearing in his first All-Star Game.

The tall left-hander watched as Boston Red Sox slugger David Ortiz strode up to home plate. Ortiz is one of the most feared batters in baseball. He waved his bat like a weapon. Clayton wound up and threw a **fastball** past Ortiz. The pitch went 95 miles per hour, smacking into the catcher's mitt.

After two more blazing fastballs, Clayton fooled Ortiz with a **slider**. The mighty Ortiz swung and missed. Strikeout!

New York Yankee Robinson Cano was next. He had won the Home Run Derby the night before, bashing a total of 32 baseballs into the stands. Cano dug into the batter's

Clayton aims and fires, showing perfect form at the 2011 All-Star Game.

box and waited for a pitch he could blast. He never got it. Instead, Clayton threw a **curveball** that broke down so much that it looked like it was rolling off a table. Cano grounded out weakly to first base.

The third batter was Detroit Tiger catcher Alex Avila, who would go on to win the Silver Slugger award that year. Avila also hit a ground ball to first base.

Clayton had pitched a perfect inning, beating three of the best American League batters. He would remember that moment for the rest of his life.

Clayton made many friends when he was on Dodgers' minor league teams. Here he is with the Great Lakes Loons in June 2007, trying to work his way up to the majors.

Becoming the One

Clayton Edward Kershaw was born on March 19, 1988, in Dallas, Texas. His mother is Marianne Kershaw. He is her only child. He writes in his book *Arise: Live Out Your Faith and Dreams on Whatever Field You Find Yourself* that he was given "the gift of being born to such a great mother."

Clayton's father, Christopher George Clayton Kershaw, is an award-winning musician. He divorced Marianne when Clayton was 10 years old.

Clayton grew up in an **affluent** part of Dallas known as Highland Park. He writes, "Though I lived with just my mom, I felt like I had 10 different homes. . . . For me, family includes friends."

9

He loved being outdoors. He played soccer, hockey, and football. But his first love was playing Little League baseball with his best friends.

When Clayton was in his first year at Highland Park High School, one of his teachers asked the class to share their dreams of what they wanted to be. Clayton said that he wanted to play professional baseball. The teacher told him that the odds against that were a million to one. Then he added, "But the important thing is that you see yourself as the one. . . . Be the one." Those words **inspired** Clayton to make that dream a goal.

It helped that he lived in Highland Park, which was well-known for its sports programs. "We didn't have a lot of money," Clayton told Ken Gurnick of mlb.com. "I don't know how she [his mother] did it. But keeping me in that school district, that was huge."

Clayton justified the sacrifices his mother made. His natural ability and long hours practicing made him into the one person in a million who can throw a baseball almost 100 miles per hour. Major League **scouts** flocked to Highland Park to watch him. In one game as a high school senior, he struck out all 15 batters he faced. He was named the Gatorade National Baseball Player of the Year.

He realized that he could make his dream come true.

When he was with the Loons, Clayton worked on his pitching motion. His stride toward home plate became longer, giving him more power.

Clayton proudly played for the United States in the 2007 All-Star Futures Game. The game features American minor league all-stars competing against a team of players from other countries.

The Best Feeling in the World

On June 6, 2006, Clayton's friends came to his house to watch the Major League Baseball Draft on television. Soon the phone rang. It was the general manager of the Dodgers, Ned Colletti. He told Clayton he would be the Dodgers' top choice and the seventh player taken overall. Everyone jumped for joy. Colletti signed Clayton to a contract worth $2.3 million. Any family money worries were over.

He spent almost two years in the minor leagues, getting better with every game. In May 2008 the Dodgers called, telling him to come to Los Angeles right away. Clayton was going to start his first Major League game on May 25 against the St. Louis

Heading to the mound in his first Major League start on May 25, 2008, Clayton is intense and focused.

Cardinals. More than 20 friends and family members flew to Los Angeles to watch him. He could barely sleep the night before. As Clayton strode to the mound at Dodger Stadium, he prayed, "Lord, whatever happens, be with me. Be my strength today." He has prayed before every game since then.

He struck out the first batter he faced. But soon he faced Albert Pujols, the great Cardinals hitter. Pujols smashed a double and drove in a run. Clayton's only thought was, "Man, Pujols is GOOD."

For the rest of that season and the early part of the next one, he pitched well on some days but not on others. Batters learned to stay away from his wicked curveball. The Dodgers wanted him to learn a new pitch, the slider. Slower than a fastball and faster than a curve, a slider breaks sharply just before reaching the plate. The ball moves several inches to the side and downward. Clayton quickly picked it up.

The Dodgers moved from Brooklyn, New York, to Los Angeles, California, after the 1957 season, breaking many Brooklyn fans' hearts. Clayton wears a "throwback" uniform on April 21, 2011.

Going From Good to Great

The slider helped him fool more batters more of the time. He also could control it and hit the spots he wanted to hit for strikes. It changed his life on the field.

Two events changed his life off the field after the 2010 season. On December 4, he married Ellen Melson. They had grown up together and his friends were her friends. She liked to laugh and he liked to make her laugh. They had known for a long time they wanted to be together.

A month later, in January 2011, they flew to Africa to continue Ellen's work helping orphans in Zambia. He met Hope, a young girl with a beautiful smile whose parents had died from **AIDS**. Ellen and Clayton started an organization called "Kershaw's Challenge" to raise money to build a home for Hope and others like her.

With a new purpose in life, Clayton's 2011 season was one of the best any Dodger has ever had. One reason was that according to a pitching measurement, Clayton's slider was the best in all of baseball. On September 20, he won his 20th game by beating his arch-rival, Tim Lincecum of the San Francisco Giants, for the fourth time that season. When Clayton left in the eighth inning, most fans were on their feet, cheering their young hero.

Clayton became just the 11th player since 1900 to win the National League **pitching Triple Crown**. He had the most strikeouts, 248. He had the best **earned run average** (ERA)—the average number of runs given up every nine innings—only 2.28. He tied for most wins, 21. No one was surprised when he received baseball's highest pitching award, the **Cy Young Award**.

Hometown fans give a standing ovation to their hero as he leaves a game against arch-rival San Francisco Giants on September 20, 2011. He has just beaten the Giants for the fifth time that year.

Clayton was thrilled to win his first Cy Young Award, for his great 2011 season. Cy Young was a legendary pitcher who won 511 games, a record that almost certainly will never be broken.

Showing why he is one of the best bunters on his team, Clayton uses his legs to get down to the ball's level.

He had become both a star and a leader. Ramona Shelburne of ESPNLosAngeles.com wrote, "He has not arrived alone. A team has followed."

With MLB commissioner Bud Selig and wife Ellen, Clayton (the youngest winner ever) proudly accepts the 2012 Roberto Clemente Award, named after the great Pittsburgh Pirates right fielder who lost his life bringing supplies to earthquake victims.

The Journey Continues

Clayton and Ellen published *Arise* the following year. Clayton also won the **Roberto Clemente Award** that year for his work in Zambia and with kids at risk in Dallas and Los Angeles. The award is given to the player who does the most for his community.

In 2013, Clayton's 1.83 ERA led the National League for the third straight season. He became only the third pitcher to have the best ERA three years in a row. The other two are in the **Baseball Hall of Fame**–Lefty Grove and Greg Maddux. Clayton may well be on his way.

The 2013 **playoffs** had both the highest and lowest points of his season. On October 3, he led the Dodgers to a 6-1 victory over the Atlanta Braves with 12 strikeouts. That was the most strikeouts by a Dodger in postseason play since Sandy Koufax struck out 15 in 1963. Manager Don Mattingly said to Mark Saxon of ESPNLosAngeles.com, "there are not many like" his ace pitcher.

A joyful Clayton high-fives and hand-slaps delighted fans after helping his team win the National League Divisional Championship on October 7, 2013.

But it was a different story on October 18, 2013, on a chilly night in Busch Stadium in St. Louis. It was the sixth game of the National League Championship Series to see which team would go on to the **World Series**. The Cardinals blasted his pitches, scoring seven runs in five innings. Clayton left the game with his head down and his glove off, staring at the grass. The Dodgers' season was over. Clayton felt he had failed.

Looking stunned as he leaves the game in only the fifth inning, Clayton's worst game of the year results in Dodgers losing the 2013 National League Championship Series to the Cardinals. Catcher and friend A.J. Ellis can only watch.

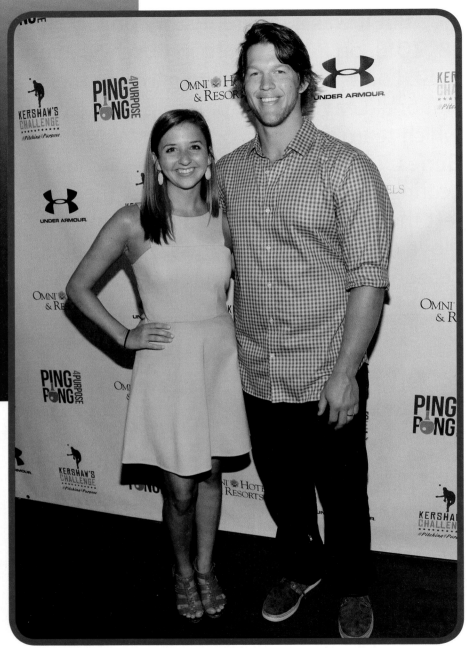

Ellen and Clayton hosted the first Ping Pong 4 Purpose Charity event, raising more money for "Kershaw's Challenge." Many Hollywood celebrities, including Jason Bateman, were there on August 29, 2013.

He told reporters, "I just wasn't good enough."

Still, he had many games when he was "good enough" during the season, which he capped by winning his second Cy Young Award. The following January, the Dodgers offered him the richest contract ever given to a pitcher, $215 million. He could have celebrated in a big way, but instead he had some friends over for ping pong and burgers. As always, he was humble and hungry.

Clayton justified the Dodgers' huge investment in the 2014 season when he threw a **no-hitter** against the Colorado Rockies on June 18. He made history: his is the only no-hitter ever with at least 15 strikeouts and no walks.

The Kershaws dedicated *Arise* to "young readers who have big dreams that are worth chasing. We are on that journey with you." For Clayton Kershaw, the journey continues.

STATISTICS

YEAR	GS	CG	W	L	ERA	IP	SO	BB	AVG
2008	21	0	5	5	4.26	107.2	100	52	.265
2009	30	0	8	8	2.79	171.0	185	91	.200
2010	32	1	13	10	2.91	204.1	212	81	.214
2011	33	5	21	5	2.28	233.1	248	54	.207
2012	33	2	14	9	2.53	227.2	229	63	.210
2013	33	3	16	9	1.83	236.0	232	52	.195
*2014	18	5	13	2	1.82	128.1	157	17	.200

*Stats as of August 6, 2014
GS = Games started; CG = Complete games; W = Wins; L = Losses; ERA = Earned run average; IP = Innings pitched; SO = Strikeouts; BB = Bases on balls; AVG = Opponents' batting average

CHRONOLOGY

1988 Clayton Edward Kershaw is born on March 19, in Dallas, Texas.

2006 Clayton is named Gatorade National Baseball Player of the Year and drafted by the Los Angeles Dodgers.

2007 Clayton pitches in the minor leagues.

2008 Starts his first game for the Dodgers on May 25.

2009 Clayton develops a slider, which makes him much more effective as a pitcher.

2010 Clayton marries Ellen Melson.

2011 The Kershaws travel to Zambia to help orphans; Clayton pitches in his first All-Star Game and wins the Cy Young Award at the end of the season.

2012 Clayton and his wife Ellen publish *Arise: Live Out Your Faith and Dreams on Whatever Field You Find Yourself*.

2013 Wins second Cy Young Award.

2014 Signs contract worth $215 million in January, becoming the highest-paid pitcher in Major League Baseball; throws a no-hitter on June 18.

FIND OUT MORE

Books

Dzidrums, Christine and Joseph Dzidrums. *Clayton Kershaw: Pitching Ace*. Whittier, CA: Creative Media Publishing, 2014.

Kershaw, Clayton, and Ellen Kershaw. *Arise: Live Out Your Faith and Dreams on Whatever Field You Find Yourself*. Ventura, CA: Regal/Gospel Light, 2011.

On the Internet

Clayton Kershaw, Major League Baseball
   http://mlb.mlb.com/team/player.jsp?player_id=477132#gameType=%27R%27

Kershaw's Challenge
   http://www.kershawschallenge.com

Los Angeles Dodgers: Kids
   http://losangeles.dodgers.mlb.com/la/fan_forum/kids_index.jsp

Works Consulted

Bonsignore, Vincent. "Clayton Kershaw a Shadow of His Former Self." *San Bernardino County Sun*, October 19, 2013.

————. "Young Gun Dodgers' Kershaw Captures Award as National League's Top Pitcher." *Daily News* (Los Angeles), November 18, 2011.

Eichenberger, Bill. "Q & A with Dodgers SP Clayton Kershaw." *The Sporting News*, July 18, 2009.

Gurnick, Ken. "Kershaw not afraid to reach for new heights." mlb.com, October 2, 2013. http://mlb.mlb.com/news/article/la/dodgers-clayton-kershaw-not-afraid-to-reach-for-new-heights?ymd=20131001&content_id=62314752

Hoffarth, Tom. "The secret to Cy success for the Dodgers' Kershaw: His wife, Ellen, and their challenging missions to Zambia." *Daily News* (Los Angeles), January 17, 2012. http://www.insidesocal.com/tomhoffarth/2012/01/17/the-secret-to-s/

Jackson, Tony. "Clayton Kershaw: The Stuff of Legend?" ESPNLosAngeles.com, August 4, 2011.

————. "Kershaw Has Reason To Celebrate." *Daily News* (Los Angeles), March 29, 2009.

FIND OUT MORE

Keown, Tim. "Anything You Can Do..." *ESPN The Magazine*, March 27, 2012.

Keri, Jonah. "The Growing Legend of Clayton Kershaw." Grantland. com, May 8, 2013. http://grantland.com/features/clayton-kershaw-best-pitcher-league-blasphemy-compare-sandy-koufax/

Knight, Molly. "Kershaw: Koufax Is a Great Teacher." *ESPN The Magazine*, December 1, 2011.

Painter, Jill. "Dodgers Roll on I-5." *Daily News* (Los Angeles), June 22, 2009.

———. "It's All Smiles For Kershaw in Debut MLB: Rookie Left-hander Pitches Well as Dodgers Beat Cardinals." *Daily News* (Los Angeles), May 26, 2008.

Saxon, Mark. "Kershaw Doesn't Leave Dodgers Short." ESPNLosAngeles.com, October 8, 2013.

———."Kershaw Launches Dodgers into October." ESPN.com, October 3, 2013.

Schoenfield, David. "Cardinals Blast Kershaw to Head to Series." ESPN.com, October 18, 2013.

Shelburne, Ramona. "Clayton Kerhsaw Has Arrived." ESPNLosAngeles.com, September 25, 2011.

Sports Illustrated Kids. "Dodger Ace Clayton Kershaw Builds Homes, Hope, and a Legacy," June 27, 2013. http://www.sikids. com/althetes-give-back/clayton-kershaw-builds-homes-hope-and-legacy

Verducci, Tom. "My Sportsman: Clayton Kershaw." SI.com, November 29, 2012.

Werner, Joseph. "Comparing Greatness: Kershaw vs. Koufax." ESPN. com, November 12, 2013.

GLOSSARY

affluent (aa-FLEW-uht)–Well-off, wealthy.

AIDS (AYDZ)–Acquired Immune Deficiency Syndrome, an often-fatal disease caused by a virus.

Baseball Hall of Fame–A museum in Cooperstown, New York, honoring players who are voted in by baseball writers.

curveball (KURV-bahl)–A pitch that spins so much that the stitches of the ball cut through the air, making it fall to one side.

Cy Young Award–An award named for a famous pitcher, honoring the best pitcher in both the American League and National League as determined by a vote of baseball writers.

earned run average (ERA)–the average number of runs a pitcher gives up for every nine innings he pitches. It does not include runs scored because of errors.

fastball (FAAST-bahl)–A straight pitch thrown as hard as a pitcher can throw.

inspired (inn-SPYURD)–Made someone want to do something.

Major League Baseball Draft–The annual selection of eligible players by all Major League Baseball teams.

no-hitter (no-HIT-tuhr)–A game in which the opposing team doesn't get any base hits.

pitching Triple Crown–An award for having the most strikeouts, the lowest ERA, and the most wins in a single season.

playoffs (PLAY-ahfs)–After the regular season is over, the teams with the best records play to see who will be in the World Series.

Roberto Clemente Award–An award named after the Pittsburgh Pirates player killed in a plane crash while bringing help to earthquake victims in Nicaragua, presented to the player who has done the most for his community.

scouts (SKOUTZ)–People who travel to watch players to see if they are good enough to be signed to a contract.

Silver Slugger–Award given annually to the best offensive player at each position in both the American and National Leagues.

slider (SLY-duhr)–A pitch slower than a fastball and faster than a curve, which breaks sharply just before reaching home plate.

World Series–The final set of games between the American League and National League champions to determine the world champion. The team that wins four games out of seven is the winner.

INDEX